The Husband From Hell

THE HUSBAND FROM HELL

Peter Kins

EXCELLER BOOKS®
A GLOBAL PRESS

The Husband from Hell

Cover by Exceller Books using resources from Pixabay.com

ISBN: 978-81-19524-22-8

Published in India in 2025 by Exceller Books,
An imprint of GE Group

Address: G1, Dream Apartment, Degree College Road, Belgharia,
Kolkata, 700056, India
www.excellerbooks.com

EXCELLER BOOKS®
A GLOBAL PRESS

Acknowledgement

I wish to acknowledge all those who assisted me in one way or another to accomplish the task of writing this book. First, let me acknowledge my wife, Regina W. Gathata for her support during the writing of this book. Next, I acknowledge Florence Juna for her good job of typing my manuscript. Next, I thank Martin Otito for his excellent job of making sure that my manuscript reached the publishers in the correct format. Lastly but not the least, the staff of Exceller Books who have made this book possible despite my unjustified impatience.

Table of Contents

Chapter 1

This is the story of a young lady called Susan Shiro and her husband, Charles Budda. I have told it as she narrated it to me verbatim.

This is her story in her own words:

What I am about to tell you is the story of my turbulent marriage. Actually, calling my relationship with my ex-husband marriage will do an injustice to the institution of marriage. I can only term ours as a catastrophe, a union made in hell.

It all started one gloomy evening, drizzling, windy, and chilly. The bus stop was becoming darker and darker, and I was becoming increasingly worried. The bus was late, and I was all alone in that desolate place. Then suddenly, the headlights of an approaching vehicle raised my spirits. *The bus is finally here* - I told myself. As the vehicle approached, I realized it was not the bus but a private car. It zoomed past like a race car, and my heart sank.

Ten minutes later, another approaching vehicle had my spirits soar again. But as the vehicle neared the bus stop, I was dismayed to realize that, again, it was not the bus; it was a private car, but this one was not speeding; in fact, it was slowing. It stopped right in front of me, and the driver rolled down the passenger window and asked, "Want a ride, lady?" I could not see the driver, and I was not going to accept a ride from a stranger at that time of evening.

"No, thanks," I blurted out. I was scared and ready to bolt if he attempted to get out of the car.

"Ma'am, I'm a pastor, and I only want to help you out of this dangerous place," he said soothingly, "Here is my card." He waved a business card at me. For a moment, I was lost and confused. On one hand, I was desperate to get out of that bleak place, and on the other hand, this was a total stranger.

"Get in; you can get pneumonia in that rain," he said to me, throwing the door open for me.

"Please put on the cabin light; I want to see you." My voice was quivering with fear. Without hesitation, he switched on the cabin light, lighting up the car. I was taken aback to see an exceptionally smart man in a Stuart Hughes suit, fully studded with jewels. His handsome face was shining in the light.

"Come in," he urged me on with a flashy smile that made my fear evaporate completely.

I got in beside him and slammed the door shut.

"Thanks for stopping," I said as the car started to move again. My voice was now smooth, and the quiver was gone.

He switched off the cabin light, plunging the car back into darkness. The headlight beam penetrated the darkness in the front of the car.

"My duty to humanity," he said out of the darkness. "I like helping people. I am Charles Budda; what is your name?"

I relaxed back in the seat, enjoying the warmth of the car and the sweet melody from the dashboard radio.

"I'm Susan," I said lightly, "Susan Shiro."

"Where are you heading?" he asked in his baritone voice.

"I'm going home to Ngong," I returned easily.

"Ooh…that is a bit far," he said, "I live in Karen, a few miles before you reach Ngong, but no problem, I will drive you home."

We drove in silence, but once in a while, he would ask a question about my life. He was a reserved, taciturn man. I was not talkative either.

On reaching Westland, just after Nairobi CBD, he suggested we stop for dinner. I welcomed the idea because I was starting to feel hungry.

I do not remember the name of the restaurant where we had our dinner, but I do remember it was an excellent dinner: citrus salmon and curried butternut in squash stew. We ate in silence, but we had a meaningful conversation afterwards as we enjoyed digestives. I drank red wine while he partook in a rusty nail cocktail.

According to him, he lived on the 4th floor of the apartment. He was married once, but his wife died in a car accident. His parents were deceased, and he had two siblings, a brother and a sister. He owned a real estate firm with interests across the globe, and so, in his own words, *money was and never was a problem for him.*

I noticed he was overly conceited. I also discovered he was a big liar when I enquired about the business card he had shown me to prove he was a Pastor, a man of God.

He laughed it off, saying that it was to help me trust him to get me home. I never thought much of that statement at that time, but I would remember it many months later.

Looking back, I think, at that juncture, I was mesmerized by his flashy lifestyle, and infatuation was setting in. To a 25-year-old girl like me, he was what I had always dreamed of: tall, handsome, and very rich, with big ideas.

On that first day, I made the hasty decision that if he asked me to marry him, I would readily agree. It was a crazy decision, inspired by fantasy and an immature mind. It laid the foundation for my future suffering.

I was 25 years old then, fresh from college, where I obtained a degree in pharmacology. I was yet to be placed anywhere, but I had high expectations and was ready to start my career. Unknown to me then, nature had other ideas for my life. My life was about to fall into a deep pit of destruction, but this was mercifully hidden from me. As it was, I was a youngster, eager and excited to try anything in this world. In other words, I was unconsciously ready for destruction.

We resumed our journey some minutes after 10:00 p.m., and, like before, we drove in silence for most of the time. Most of that time, I was engrossed in my fantasy world, imagining myself sharing my life with this gorgeous man. Remember, he had not even shown any romantic interest in me so far.

We arrived at our gate shortly before midnight. Before I could step out of the car, he took my hand and kissed it.

"You are a very pretty girl … I will come to see you again," he said, then released my hand, and I got out of the car. He drove off, leaving me staring at his tail lights. I was confused by his actions. It was somehow an anti-climax – ***you are a very pretty girl … I will come to see you again.***

I did not see him again for the next four weeks. There were no mobile phones then.

I was about to give up on him when, suddenly, out of nowhere, he materialized. I was leaving home one Saturday morning when I came upon his car parked a few metres from our gate. It was parked in such a way that he would never miss me if I ever got out of that gate. When he saw me, he stepped out of the car.

"Hello, pretty," he said, grinning, "I have come for you." If he intended that line to be the romantic opener, then he was quite off the mark. To me, it sounded like a command rather than a request for a date; even the way it came out was somehow condescending. I was ready for a relationship with him, but he had to show respect. I was not there for his picking; I was a woman, and he had to woo me!

"Why should you come for me?" I retorted.

He grimaced. He was obviously taken aback by my comment.

"Are you not happy to see me?" he asked sorrowfully.

"I am surprised to see you."

"Why? Don't you remember I said I would come back to see you again?" he said hoarsely.

"Yes, to see me, not to come for me!"

"Yes … yeah, true … that was a slip of the tongue," he said unsteadily, "I am here to see you … to talk to you."

I moved closer to him.

"That is better. What do you want to tell me?" I felt better that I had put him down in his place.

He grunted.

"Why don't we talk inside the car?"

"Okay," I agreed readily because I wanted to get out of the way in case my dad, who was still in the house, came out through the gate.

He courteously led me around the car to the passenger side and held the door open for me to get in. He went back to his side and settled down beside me in the front seat.

He turned his face towards me.

"I have been thinking about you since that night we were together," he said melodiously, "You can't say you just forgot all about me."

His deep, soothing voice had me in a trance. To have such a handsome and fabulously rich man interested in me had an immense effect on me.

"Thank you for thinking about me," I said, fumbling with words, "I also thought of you."

He reached out for my hand.

"You are a very sweet girl to look at," he continued, "Please allow me to take you to my house. I want you to know where I live, and then after that, I take you on a special date. Let this Saturday mark the beginning of our endless love. I will love you like you have never been loved. I will make all your dreams come true. I will give you a home and everything else money can buy. Above all, I will cherish you all days of my life."

My heart was pounding inside my chest with excitement. I knew instantly that I wanted this man for myself.

"Please let me take you home," he said softly, fondling my hand.

"Yes, let's go," I grunted. I was ready for him; I was ready for everything he said. That was how hooked I was. He pulled me towards him and kissed my forehead softly.

"Thanks, darling." He let go of my hand and started the car engine. To me, the drive to his house was like flying over the skies of sweet emotions.

He lived in an impressive townhouse in the wooded estate of Karen. He welcomed me into his house with such pomp, making me feel like royalty. Although there was no one else in the house, the way everything was laid out for me made it look like some workers had done it. The food was well prepared and preserved in thermal pots. It was so delicious-looking, and its aroma made one feel pangs of hunger.

When we were done with lunch, we shifted to the lounge, where he mixed and served red wine. He then came and sat next to me. His perfume oozed raunchy sex appeal.

"I have been thinking about this moment for a long time," he said merrily, putting his arm over my shoulders. It sent a shiver through my body.

"And why didn't you come to see me earlier?" I asked.

"I don't like rushing things," he responded.

"But don't you think you're rushing things now by putting your arm on me?" I said.

He laughed.

"No ... this is not the first time we are meeting; we are friends," he went on, trying to justify his actions. But, secretly, I was enjoying what he was doing.

"Tell me, sweetie, do you have a boyfriend?" he asked soothingly.

"No," I replied.

"Then that makes two of us," he said.

"When did your wife die?" I asked.

"Two years ago," he replied.

"And you have never got someone since then?"

"I decided to give myself a break of at least five years ... but that was before I met you."

"What happened when you met me?"

"I felt I had found my soul mate," he said, looking at my face, "I believe you are the love of my life."

I blushed.

"I feel the same," I said coyly.

That must have encouraged him, for he had put his other hand on my knee. From that moment on, I lost touch with reality. I only woke up many hours later beside him in his bed. We were both naked. I felt satiated, although I was feeling slightly guilty of having unprotected sex on the first date.

In the evening, we went to the nightclub to party. It was the first Saturday of the month, and the club was full and lively. The dance floor, with its glittering lights, was teeming with energetic dancers.

As we enjoyed our drinks, Budda suddenly blurted out, "Be careful; do not dance with that Scum." He said with a slightly raised voice, looking and gesturing towards the people on the dance floor, "They are no good!"

I was taken aback by his opinion of people he did not even know. They were just enjoying themselves.

"What is wrong with them?" I asked, looking at his face.

"They have no education, no money, just trouble!" The disgust in his voice clearly conveyed his dislike for them. I decided not to pursue the matter further, although it left me with many unanswered questions. We continued with our hushed conversion, but his harsh opinion of the other revellers had injected some hidden tension in us.

"Excuse me," he said suddenly, patting my knee. He got to his feet and headed to the washrooms.

It took just a few minutes for someone to notice I was alone. He came up to our table and politely asked me to dance with him. In the dim of our secluded table, I could not see his face clearly. All I could see was his lean, tall frame. But I heard his voice clearly over the din.

"No, please," I told him softly, remembering Budda's warning: **they have no education, no money, just trouble.** It was not that I shared the same view with him, but I did not want to annoy my new-found love.

In a desperate move to emphasize his request, he hesitantly reached out for my hand. He held it momentarily before I withdrew it. But Budda, who was just reaching our table then, saw what had happened. He grabbed the young man by his shirt's collar and shook him violently.

"Who the hell are you to touch my wife?" he demanded in a fierce voice. "Are you mad?"

The shocked man just stared at him.

In a rage, Budda slapped the intruder across his face, sending him down the small platform to the dance floor. The thin man lay quietly, his eyes shut, like he was in a coma.

Still ranting and raving, Budda made a beeline towards the defenceless man, but a mob, made up mostly of the man's friends, came to his defence, raining blows and kicks on Budda. His attempt to fight them off was met with more violent blows until he also went down and spread out on the carpet. I dragged myself out of my dazed state and went down to him; drops of blood oozed from his nose. He looked pathetic. As I was about to touch him, he sprang up to his feet.

"Let us get out of here," he said angrily, "I have had enough of this asshole!"

He paid our bill, and we left in a huff. He was still visibly angry. When we reached his house, he sat me on the sofa but remained standing, hovering over me.

"What game were you playing with that idiot at the club?" he asked me harshly.

I was thrown off balance by his accusation.

"Game … what game are you talking about?"

"Stop pretending; I saw everything; I saw you were holding hands; can you deny that, you bitch?" He cut me short, shouting at me angrily.

"I don't know what you are talking about! And stop insulting me; I'm not your wife!" I shouted back at him.

He descended on me with blows and kicks.

"No woman plays games with me and gets away with them! I will teach you that lesson tonight!"

I fell down on the carpet, and he continued kicking and punching me mercilessly. My screams did not deter him at all; he knew nobody outside the house could hear them.

He continued beating me until I lost consciousness.

A splitting headache and a throbbing pain in both my arms woke me up. I found myself alone in a fabulously furnished room. I did not know where I was, but I presumed I was still in Budda's house.

As I tried to figure out where I was, memories of the events of the previous night flooded my mind. The mental anguish was overwhelming. How could a man who said he loved me, whom I had easily yielded myself to, be so cruel? Why did he treat me so cheaply? Was it because I had given myself to him so cheaply?

At that moment, all pleasant thoughts and high esteem I had for him evaporated. I hated myself and him.

Every part of my body was aching. I pushed the bedclothes aside to view my injuries. I was still clothed. I could not see any injuries, but the pain was everywhere. I swung my feet to the floor and struggled to my feet. There was a pricking pain in my left knee; I limped to the window. The room was on the ground floor, but the window was secured with metal bars. I limped to the door and turned the handle; to my surprise, the door swung open to reveal a corridor that led to another door.

I must get out of this place now – I told myself. My heart was pounding wildly in my chest. I did not want to see that man again in my life. I saw my shoes under the bed, and my clutch bag was on the nightstand next to the bed. I hurriedly crawled under the bed, scooped my shoes, got up, snapped up my little bag, and then wobbled towards the door, but it was too late for my escape. Budda's massive shoulders blocked the door. His sight suffocated me with fright. I froze, my heart still pulsating madly.

He came forward and laid his big hands on my shoulders. "Babe, we can talk this matter over," he said soothingly, but his very sight made me sick. I hated him.

Chapter 1

"We have nothing to talk about!" I said firmly, "I don't want to ever see you again!"

I brushed off his hands and made for the door, but he held me.

"I will make it up for you. I swear," he pleaded, "I will give you whatever you want. I swear it will never happen again. I was mad at that bastard."

"That is your problem!" I said vehemently, "I don't want to ever see you again! You disgust me; leave me alone!"

The venom in my voice made him release me and step away. He looked shocked or maybe amused by my tantrum.

"Okay, okay, fine, then let me drive you home, or I call a taxi for you," he said calmly.

"No! I said I don't want anything from you." I retorted and stormed out of the room.

Three weeks passed by without much activity in my life. After I left Budda's place, I retreated to my room, where I spent most of my time drowning my sorrow by crying incessantly and listening to gospel music. It was terribly painful to know I had betrayed myself by transgressing against God in the most obnoxious sin. Having sex with a stranger I hardly knew was horrible, unthinkable.

To cover for my seclusion and limping state, I lied to my mum that I had fallen off from a moving bus. She asked if I had gone to the police to report the driver, but I told her it was my fault that I fell. She bought my story and let me be. She diligently served my food in my room. My father rarely came to my room, and when he did, he stood at the door to enquire how I was doing. I hated myself for making my parents go through the agony of watching their only daughter suffer so much pain.

By the end of week eight, I felt much better. I was healed and ready to resume my normal life. **But I was wrong; my life would never be normal again!**

Chapter 2

Two months into my 'normal life,' the bubble burst in my face. In those two months, I had forgotten my biological cycles as a woman. I remembered with profound shock that I had not received my period. Two months! I rushed to the pharmacy and bought a self-test pregnancy kit. All this time, stress and anxiety were choking me.

Back in my room, I locked the door and did the test. The two clear stripes told me clearly that I was pregnant! My head spun wildly, and I was forced to lie down on the bed to avoid falling down. Time stood still for me. My mind was blank. Fear of the future paralyzed me. I must have passed out because when I woke up again, it was dark; then I remembered the pregnancy test, and my head started to spin again. I knew I had to take control of myself, or else I would lose my mind. I had to force myself to be sober. This situation demanded critical thinking, I told myself, not whimpering.

The first thought that came to my mind was abortion, but the horror stories I had heard about procuring abortion made me dismiss that idea from my mind completely. I was not ready to die, and I was also not ready to live with the guilt of the murder of an innocent soul.

I equated abortion to covering a sin with another sin. I was ready to live with adultery or fornication but not abortion! It broke my heart to know that my child would be fatherless. How would I tell him that his biological father was a heartless monster who hurt women and loathed those he considered below his class? My relationship with that man was dead on arrival, and there was no going back.

My greatest headache now was my parents. They were respected members of our community; my mother was a member of a women's guild, and my father was a church minister. The shame I had brought them was unimaginable. I dreaded the moment I would break to them the bad news. I would have preferred to tell my father about it to my mother. My father would understand me, but our tradition forbade it, so I had to tell my mother, who would, in return, tell my father.

I knew my mother would be mad at me and turn violent. I had tasted her wrath in the past, and I knew what she was capable of, but I had a solution to reach her. I would use her mother, my grandmother, to tell her. I knew grandmother had a soothing effect on my mother.

My plan worked very well, but suddenly and unexpectedly, Budda turned up in our house and overturned my life plans again. I was not at home when he turned up, but my parents were there. When they were coming to terms with my situation, Budda had come to ask for my hand in marriage. He came in all his splendor, and in his best manners. My parents, understandably, fell for him. Here was a man willing to wipe out their shame.

On his side, Budda was over the moon to hear that I was pregnant, although nobody had told him that it was his because I had not even told my parents who the father of my baby was; he rightly assumed it was his.

"If she agrees, then we, as her parents, have no problem with you marrying her," my father told him.

When I came home later that evening, even without being told, I could sense something in the air.

"Shiro!" my mother called me from my room.

I went to the sitting room, where they were waiting for me.

"Sit down," my mother went on, "Your friend was here."

I sat down.

"Which one?"

"He told us his name is Charles Budda. Do you know him?"

My heart did a summersault!

"I don't know him," I returned defensively. "I don't have such a friend."

Father grunted.

"Are you sure of that?" his voice was calm, "He told us that you are his lover."

"He is not my lover!"

It felt awful discussing Budda with my parents.

"So you know him?" Father asked.

"Yes, I know him, but I don't want to talk about him. He is not my friend."

"How do you know him?"

"I met him some time ago, but we did not get along well."

"He told us that he loves you very much ... and you should forgive him for the misunderstanding that happened between you two."

I could not believe what I was hearing — a **misunderstanding between you two!** That was the understatement of the year. He nearly killed me, and he dared call it a misunderstanding.

"I don't love him, and I don't want anything to do with him," I said firmly, "Tell him I'm not interested in his love. I don't even want to see him!"

My father sighed.

"Okay, my daughter, tell us what happened," he said soothingly.

"Nothing happened, I simply don't want anything to do with that man," I said impatiently, getting to my feet, "I'm going to my room."

There was no way I was going to tell my parents that I had unprotected sex with a stranger. No, never!

They watched in consternation as I walked out of the room, not knowing what to do. I felt like a heel, subjecting my innocent parents to all the anguish.

Three days later, Budda ambushed me at our gate, and although I flatly refused to enter his car, he still managed, on his knees, to convince me to listen to him.

"Shiro, babe ... please give me a chance to explain myself," he pleaded, still kneeling before me. "Sorry, I let anger get the better of me on that day."

"How did I make you angry?"

"No, darling, you didn't make me angry at all," he said, looking up at me, his eyes teary, "As I have just said, it was wrong for me to let anger drive me to do such a horrible thing to you, my love. Please understand me, you are the love of my life, and something like that will never happen again. I swear to God, just give me another chance to make it up for you. I promise to love you forever and ever…"

"I don't want your love." I cut him short, "I'm no longer interested in you."

"Sweetie … don't throw this chance away; you and I can go far; I have everything you need in your life. I have endless love for you and a lot of money to spend on you. I swear I will never touch you again … I mean, I will never beat you again. Never, never, just give me another chance."

It was at that point my heart began to thaw.

"Are you sure of what you are telling me?" I asked. I was still skeptical.

I knew he knew he had won me over.

"Darling, don't doubt me. I wouldn't have gone to your parents if I wasn't sure," he said soothingly, "I need you in my life. You have won my heart over. I am in love with you."

"Thank you, but I need time to think about it," I said calmly, "Do you know I'm pregnant?"

"Yes, and I'm so happy; you know my late wife never gave me a baby! I am overly excited. I'm going to be a father!" he said excitedly.

"But who told you it is yours?" I asked him lightly.

He grinned.

"A man can always tell when he has hit the bull's eye; a healthy baby-carrying ejaculation is always voluminous. I knew even before your parents told me. Thanks for making me a father!" he said with a mirth.

"Okay, I have nothing more to say for now," I said, "I will see you some other time."

"Can I drop you somewhere?"

"No, I will manage."

"I will be here to see you ... same time next Saturday. I love you!" he said, getting to his car. He drove off, leaving me dazed and confused.

For the next week, my mind was in a state of disturbance, confusion and uncertainty. I was confronted by two not-so-pleasant options: Reject or accept Budda's marriage proposal; both of them had serious repercussions. Rejecting him would mean raising my unborn baby alone with all the challenges that come with parenting. On the other hand, accepting him would mean risking my life. I had serious reservations about living with someone with his kind of temper. I knew every time we disagreed, he would turn violent. I had no doubt about that.

After three organizing days, I decided to consult my mother. I wanted her to help me make a decision. I came clear and told her everything, not caring what she thought of me. She listened attentively without interrupting me. When I was done, she sighed and said, "Sorry, my child, in life, most of the time, we don't get what we desire, but we still soldier on with what we get." She paused and then went on after a moment. "Tell me, what is your feeling towards this man?"

"I sincerely don't know," I said softly, "At the beginning, I was quite ecstatic to start a life with him, but after he beat me so ruthlessly, I'm no longer sure."

"I'm of the opinion that you should give him a second chance, but with one strict condition," Mother went on.

"What condition?" I asked anxiously.

She fidgeted.

"If he ever lays his hands on you again, even once, you get out for good." The emphasis in her words and voice was enough to convince me that was the way to go about it. If he could hold on to that condition, everything would work out alright for me.

My father summoned Budda to our house for a reconciliation meeting. It was a friendly meeting, and Budda accepted all the conditions and terms my father had spelt out to him. He swore never to hurt me again, and as usual, his charm won the day. We all accepted his marriage proposal, and that is how I came to marry Charles Budda, my tormentor.

Our wedding was held at the registrar's office, attended by a few friends and relatives. A simple reception ceremony at home brought down the curtains. It was not the kind of wedding one would have expected of someone of Budda's stature. It was like he somehow did not take our union seriously. I was not happy about it.

We did not go on a honeymoon. Budda claimed he had a very important business engagement that could not be delayed, but he argued that the honeymoon could be deferred to another time.

Our married life began in low-key mode, not what I would have expected of newly wedded. It took me just a fortnight to discover that my husband's sexual appetite was far above mine. He wanted sex every day, sometimes several times. I found it tiring and boring. For me, I wanted more romance and less sex. This incompatibility worried me; it was a red alert. Apart from his excessive sexual demands, he treated me fairly well. My pregnancy progressed well without any complications. On the 40th week, I delivered a baby boy; he named him Peter Sonko.

It was after the birth of my baby that the demons in my husband emerged. I was discharged from the hospital two days after delivery. My husband came to pick us up; he was very jovial, and the sight of his son seemed to excite him. When we got home, he excused himself, saying he had some urgent matters to attend to. He left us alone under the care of the house help. He returned around midnight, drunk and rowdy. I was awakened by his meaningless oinking and the loud cracking of the floorboards as he stumbled upstairs.

He burst into the bedroom noisily, without a thought for the sleeping baby. It was the first time I saw him so drunk. It was a frightful sight. The foul smell of alcohol hit me, making me feel nauseous.

Chapter 2

"Shiro! Get up! Your husband is here!" he bellowed. I ignored him. It took him around twenty minutes to take off his clothes and put on his pajamas. He then slid under the bedclothes, still muttering to himself. His first mission in the bed was to have sex with me. I was appalled. This was my first day from the hospital after delivering a baby, and I was still stitched down there. I pushed off his groping hand, and that seemed to infuriate him, for he immediately turned rough. He tore my pantie and threw it away together with the absorbent cotton wool. He then forced himself on me, causing me so much pain. I cried beneath him as he raped me. It was the worst form of violation I had ever gone through. When he was done, he slumped beside me and began to snore almost immediately. The sight of him made me sick. I felt so hurt and humiliated. I got out of bed, picked up my baby and went to the guest room.

That was the longest night of my life; physical and emotional pain could not let me sleep. I felt like ending my life, but the life of my baby held me back. At that point in my life, I felt worthless. How could my husband violate me in such a horrible way! It sent a clear message to me that I meant nothing to him.

In the morning, he did not come to see us; I had just heard his car drive off. During the many hours I stayed awake throughout the night, I thought of quitting. I did not love him anymore, but for the sake of my baby, I changed my mind. It was a big mistake on my part.

For the next two weeks, we ignored each other. The house help did all the household chores while I concentrated on baby care.

Then all of a sudden, he started talking and treating me as if he loved me, but I was skeptical and continued ignoring him. My subconscious mind kept telling me that he was not genuine. He was just trying to cover up his heinous crime, but he was still the same beast I had come to know. I knew he was still a danger to me, no matter how much he pretended otherwise. I also started doubting his state of mental health as who, in his normal state of mind, would rape his wife, who had just given birth? It did not make sense to me.

I later discovered that he was trying to be good to me so I could start giving him sex, but that was quite difficult for me; it would take a long time to heal, both physically and emotionally. I felt nothing for him. Although I had returned to the master bedroom, I did not let him touch me, nor did he try to force himself on me again.

Just when I thought our marriage life was returning to normal, I was rudely disillusioned. This is how it happened. On that day, a Saturday, he arrived home at around 8 p.m., which was unusual because his return time on Saturdays was always after midnight. He came into the house and ordered the house help to prepare the guest room in the basement for his guests.

"Where is the visitor?" I enquired curiously.

"Outside, in the car," he said curtly and walked out of the room. I suspected to avoid more questions and went to the window to see the mysterious visitor.

Budda went back to the car, got into the passenger seat, and shut the door. There was a person in the passenger seat, but I could not see him/her from where I was standing behind the bedroom window.

Fifteen minutes later, Budda got out of the car, walked around the car to the passenger's side and opened the door for his visitor to get out. My heart kicked violently when I saw her. Her face makeup radiated in the powerful landscape lighting. She wore a blue mini-skirt that hugged her figure tightly. Her white top just hung over her huge breasts, leaving her belly exposed. She was very young, maybe 20 years old, and extremely gorgeous. Her attractiveness filled me with envy, jealousy and uncontrollable rage. Budda had now crossed the red line, and I was boiling with violent emotions. I was now ready for anything!

Budda held her hand and guided her towards the main entrance of the house. I ran downstairs and positioned myself at the upper entrance of the basement as the two love birds turned into the corridor leading to the basement. When Budda saw me, anger appeared on his face. They came closer, still holding hands.

"What are you doing here, blocking the way?" he demanded harshly.

"I will not allow her anywhere in this house!" I said hoarsely.

"And who are you to do that?" he asked with a condescending sneer in his voice.

"I'm your wife and mother of your baby!" I retorted violently.

I saw the girl's head jerk.

"Babe, you are married with a baby?" There was disbelief in her voice.

"No, I'm not married, babe; I will explain later," he said, and then, moving swiftly, came for me, shoving me aside.

"Get out of the way, woman, before I hurt you!" he shouted.

"I said I will not let her into this house!" I shouted back.

The back of his hand landed across my eyes, sending me down onto the floor; I lay there stunned. He held the girl by her shoulders and, stepping over me, guided her downstairs into the basement. I heard him come up the stairs; he slid the bolt across the door and went down again. His night was now secured. He had won against me and the girl. Down there, she was under his mercy. He could do anything with her; the rooms down there were soundproof. When I had calmed down, I got to my feet and lurched to the main bedroom. I lay there on the bed. I was still dazed.

I was awakened from my stupor by the yelling of my baby, and I felt scared and confused. I suckled my baby back to sleep. After I had put the baby back in his cradle, I lay on the bed to meditate, but a cloud of gloom enveloped my mind, making clear thinking almost impossible. *What had I gotten myself into in this marriage?* I kept asking myself. I knew deep in me that quitting was the solution, but I was not ready for it. I wanted to finish what I had started. I felt I could change this man to commit to our marriage.

I knew it was wishful thinking, but I kept my hopes alive. I tried to figure out what was happening in the basement, but the images that came into my mind only increased my mental anguish. The thought of my husband in bed with that sexy girl was like a knife in my heart. I really longed to fall asleep, but it was impossible. The pain in my heart was too much to allow me to sleep. I had been in this marriage for less than one year, but it felt like I had been in it for ages. I was emotionally drained. Budda had betrayed me beyond words; bringing another woman into our house was the ultimate betrayal.

The following day, Sunday, Budda and his lover remained holed up in the basement. None of them came up for anything; this was possible because the rooms in the basement were fully furnished and equipped with everything. There were refrigerators fully stocked with food and drinks. Two people could stay down there for up to two weeks without needing to come to the main house.

The next day, Monday, I saw Budda leave; he did not come to the main house; he just walked to his car and drove off; he was alone. I presumed the young girl was still in the basement, and I decided to go see her, but the upper door to the basement was still locked. I stood there, cursing Budda and the girl. I went back to the house and decided to call the phone in the basement. During those days, there were no mobile phones. I dialed the basement number, but the phone was disconnected. It was obvious Budda anticipated such a move from me and had taken precautions by disconnecting the phone. I wondered if she was there of her own volition or had been taken as a prisoner. It was impossible to tell, but I found it hard to believe that such a gorgeous and outgoing girl could agree to remain alone in a house doing nothing all day. It was obvious he had not disclosed to her that he was married. He must have deceived her that he was a bachelor or a widower, and she had swallowed it hook, line and sinker. Now she was in trouble, just like I was! I could feel it in me; an eerie atmosphere hung over the house.

That evening, Budda did not return to the house at his usual weekday time. At around midnight, I heard his car drive into the compound. I jumped out of bed and went to the window to see what was happening. I was in time to see Budda get out of the car and walk towards the house. He walked in as the gateman closed the gate. I remained there at the window to see if anything new would unfold. A few minutes later, I watched in amazement as the car was driven around the house to the back. I ran down to the sitting room window facing the backyard. Budda's car was parked in the shadows next to the house. Budda himself had already sneaked back into the basement, using a jib door, which I never knew existed. It was cleverly concealed to appear like a part of the wall of the house.

About ten minutes later, just as I was about to conclude that I was making things up, I saw Budda carrying a heavy load over his shoulder; it was wrapped in a blanket. It took me a few seconds to realize what had happened, and I had to restrain myself from screaming; he was carrying the body of a human being, and that human being could only be the girl he had brought home last night. So Budda was not only a cheater and wife-beater but also a brutal murderer.

What was I supposed to do? I wondered. Should I report to the police? Or should I call them right away? No, I told myself, I had to be sure of my facts first. If I called the police and it turned out I was wrong, I would be in trouble.

I watched in horror as Budda squeezed his 'Load' into the car boot. When he was done, he slammed the boot door shut. He then got behind the wheel and drove off.

Chapter 3

Standing there, I felt the need to share what I had witnessed with someone, but who? Ruth, the house help? Could I trust her? I thought about it and decided against it. I didn't know her well, I concluded to myself. I decided to be patient and wait to see what would happen the next day.

But nothing happened. The next day, Budda came home and pretended everything was normal, like nothing significant had happened, but I needed answers.

"We need to talk," I told him after seeing his nonchalant attitude.

He grimaced.

"Talk about what?" he retorted, "What is eating you?"

"I want to know what I'm doing in this house."

"What a question is that?" There was a grim expression on his face. "You are here because you belong here."

"As who?"

"My wife, of course."

"I remember you denied me in front of your lover; you said you were not married."

"That's the problem with you; you assume too much. First, who told you she is my lover?"

"You don't spend a night in the same bed with someone if he/she is not your lover."

"Now understand this, that lady was … is my business partner. I behaved the way I did because of your insinuation. I got angry when you assumed she was my lover."

"What did you want me to think if you didn't want me to see her? What business were you conducting holed up in the basement? I'm not that stupid." I was starting to get agitated.

"Now know, she was not my lover, and we didn't sleep together … she meant … I mean … she means nothing to me."

"Why do you keep referring to her in the past tense?"

"Nothing, just confusion, grammar error."

"Where is she now?"

He grunted.

"You must be very obsessed with her! I told you she is nothing to me, and I don't know where she is."

"Yes, at least I believe she is nothing to you."

"What do you mean?"

"If someone is past tense, then she can't be anything to anyone!"

He sighed.

"I didn't say she is past tense, whatever you mean by that." There was a tinge of anxiety in his voice. "Can we please stop discussing her?"

"Why is the basement still locked?"

"Again, you assume too much. It is not locked. I want you to tell Ruth to clean up the place tomorrow," he said, getting to his feet.

I now knew almost for sure the girl was dead. But I needed evidence to act on. So, I decided that the next day, before telling Ruth to clean up the place, I would first go there and look for evidence.

The following morning, as soon as I saw the gateman closing the gate after Budda had driven off, I headed down to the basement. The first thing I noticed was that only one of the bedrooms was used, which meant Budda had lied to me that they had not slept together. But it made my evidence-searching work much easier because now I had only one room to search. After one hour of searching, I found nothing incriminating; it seemed Budda had beaten me to it. I concluded he had searched the place himself to ensure he left nothing to incriminate him.

Then, as I was about to give up, I remembered something I had once read in a detective novel, blood stains of the victim can be splashed in the most unlikely places, like behind the curtains, underside the bed or anywhere very unlikely to search. With that information, I became more determined to search for more evidence to fix Budda. He had caused me so much pain, and now, it was my turn to cut him down to size. I got down to my knees and crawled under the bed. I had with me a powerful torch which brightly illuminated the underneath.

Underneath one of the bed frames was a thick, dried blood stain; a casual search would have never revealed that. It was a blood stain, alright, but was it the mysterious girl's blood? That I could not tell, but I assumed it was. That evidence was strong enough to crucify Budda; Kimetto, the gateman, Ruth, the house help, and I had seen Budda go in with the girl, and the blood stain was a piece of evidence strong enough to convince any court of law of Budda's guilt.

Then, suddenly, I saw the bedroom door being slowly pushed open. There was something ominous about how it was being done; whoever it was did not want to make a sound. I hurriedly crawled out of the bed, but the door swung wide open as I got to my feet. It was Budda, and my heart froze with fright.

"What are you doing down here with a torch? What are you looking for?" He boomed with anger, still holding onto the door.

"Nothing in particular," I replied shakily.

He slammed the door shut and then rushed at me; he thrust his body against mine, and we fell onto the bed.

"I told you to mind your own business, but you seem determined to wreck my life!" he grunted, squeezing my neck, "I must kill you today!"

I knew he meant to kill me like he had killed the girl.

"Please spare my life; our baby needs me," I pleaded with him.

He increased pressure on my windpipe, and I began to gasp for air.

A soft knock on the door made him ease the pressure on my neck.

"Who is it?" he shouted.

The door swung open, and Ruth, the house help, entered, carrying her cleaning equipment. She gasped. Budda swung off me and got up to his feet.

"What do you want?" he asked her angrily and then said, "Get out!"

Ruth scrambled out of the room.

"And you," he said, turning towards me, "You are lucky today, but stop poking your nose in my personal affairs! Stick to your lane! Being my wife doesn't warrant you to interfere with everything I do. I don't like it. Next time, I may not be this lenient. I can kill you … you know."

The menace in his voice sent a shiver down my spine. He turned and stomped out of the room. I was quite shaken but relieved I had cheated death by a whisker. But now my stay in his house needed serious review. Every day I stayed there, my life was in grave danger. I was now almost sure he was suffering from some kind of mental disorder, most likely bipolar disorder. I had to get out, but to where? Going back home as a single mother was something I wished to avoid at all costs. I had no money to rent my own house. Renting my own house was the best option. I could also start a business. But where was the money to set myself up? It was Budda who had put me in this quagmire, and so it was quite natural to use him to get myself out! After all, our son was the heir apparent of his wealth.

After much thought, I came up with a master plan. I would risk more time in his house as I activated my plan. It was now just a matter of time. But I was wrong; I had not reckoned with Budda's unpredictability. The events that followed could not have allowed me to activate anything against him. The happenings of the subsequent days left everyone in our household, including Budda himself, in a spin. First, he went missing for three days, and when he resurfaced, he was under heavy security of the homicide police unit. The police explained to me that my husband was the last person seen with a girl who had since gone missing. They had arrested him as their prime suspect; they were now doing their investigations and wanted to search our house for any evidence. They searched the whole house, but they found nothing incriminating. As Budda stood there, subdued, it occurred to me that I now had him in a corner. I had evidence the police were looking for, and just a word from me, Budda would be ruined completely. I decided to remain mum for now. The evidence I had against him was my secret weapon; if he laid his hands on me again, I would go to the police and tell them he killed that girl. Murder was a very serious crime. His freedom and life were now in my hands. One word from me, and it was over for him.

When they were done with their search, they bundled Budda back into their car and drove off.

For the next one month, they locked him up at the local police station. I visited him every day to offer him moral support as his wife. They released him on the 30th day due to lack of evidence.

The judge ordered that the police were free to rearrest him should they ever find any evidence against him. He came back home quite dejected. When I asked him what really happened, he told me that he did not want to talk about it, saying his business rivals were trying to frame him. I knew he was lying, but I pretended to believe him. What I knew about the missing girl was my ace, my ultimate card.

For the next six months, he behaved so well that he nearly convinced me that he had changed his character. During that period, he appeared remorseful. But, as they say, looks can be deceitful. History was about to repeat itself.

One Saturday evening, he sneaked another woman into the house using the side door at the back of the house. I only came to know about it two days later through Ruth, the house help. She furtively slipped into my bedroom.

"There is a woman in the basement," she said a little hoarsely, "She kept glancing at the door. She was slightly shaking with fear and excitement. I have seen her."

My heart lurched.

"Are you sure?" my voice was trembling.

"I have even talked to her," she returned.

"Can I go down there and see her?"

"Yes, she is alone."

"I'm going down there," I said, my mind seething with anger. Budda was now pushing me to the limit, and, unfortunately for him, I was ready and capable of bringing him down. Enough was enough. I was now ready to have him locked inside for many years. I held the trump card. I felt powerful, but anger in me was driving me mad.

I got the lady sitting on the edge of the bed; her head was bent down, admiring her manicure. She heard movement, and she looked up. Her hair was disheveled, and there were black rings around her eyes. She looked scared, not necessarily by me, but by something else. There was something about her face that made her look terrified. I approached her slowly.

"Hello, Madam … who are you?" I asked her, standing before her.

"I'm Betrice," she answered.

"And what are you doing here?"

She blinked.

"I don't know," she said softly.

"What do you mean you don't know?"

"I don't know how I ended up in this room. I remember having drinks with a man who had befriended me in the club, and then I found myself here. I think he spiked my drink."

"When was that?"

"Saturday night."

"Did you know him before that?"

"No, I had never seen him before."

"What have you been doing here since Saturday because today is Monday?"

"He has been having sex with me … telling me that I was now his wife." Her voice quivered as she talked. "But I don't want him; I want to go home."

"Where is your home?"

"I am from Nakuru, but I stay in Kasarani."

"Do you have children?"

"Yes, two. I left them with my mother and the house girl."

"How old are you?"

"I'm 30 years old."

"Did this man who brought you here tell you that he is married?"

"Yes, he did," she said truthfully, "But wanted a second wife because his first wife hates him."

It was unbelievable that Budda could do this kind of thing again. I now had a co-wife without any notice, ceremony or courtesy. Budda had betrayed me again, but this was going to be the last betrayal. His time of mischief was over. I was now ready to destroy him. The following morning, I would go to the police and tell them what I knew about the missing girl and that I had evidence that Budda had murdered the girl. I hoped that they would act on that information immediately.

"I can help you escape from here," I said, feeling pity for her.

"I would love that very much," she said softly, "Where is here?"

"Here is Karen; have you ever heard of it?"

"Yes, I know Karen Shopping Centre on the way to Ngong'."

"You are right ... I will let you out tomorrow morning if my husband, I mean your captor, will not be around."

"Thanks, Ma'am," she said mildly, "Are you his first wife?"

"No, I am his only wife."

"Okay, happy to hear that. Is it true you hate him?"

"No, I don't hate him, although I have no reason to love him."

"He is...," heavy footsteps on floorboards cut our conversation short.

We remained transfixed on our respective positions as Budda stomped into the room. He was visibly drunk.

"What are you doing here?" he asked me harshly, "I told you to stop meddling in my affairs!"

"When you bring another woman here, it also becomes my affair!" I returned fearlessly. I felt no fear of him.

"She is not another woman!" he continued, "She is my second wife; put that into your head and learn to live with it!"

"Never! Over my dead body," I said and stomped out of the room.

Back in my room, I tried the phone again, but it was still dead. It now meant I would have to personally visit the local police station to activate Budda's arrest. It was not that I was proud of betraying him, but he had pushed me to the wall.

As I sat down to plan for the following day, a notice on the TV caught my attention. The family of Patricia Mode, the girl who had gone missing and led to the arrest of Budda, was offering one million shillings for anyone who had information on the whereabouts of their loved one. I felt pity for them; I knew the kind of agony they were going through. But what they did not know was that more pain awaited them ahead. Their daughter was dead.

At the end of the notice, they gave a telephone number to call if anyone had information about her whereabouts. I jotted down the number. I thought it was easier and more effective to call the family than the police. I was not interested in the one million shillings. I just wanted Budda out of my life. I knew the police could not ignore the family, but they could ignore me. I decided to go to the Karen Mall that morning to call the family.

Chapter 4

Later, at around midnight, Budda came to our bedroom and slipped in beside me. His touch made me recoil. I could tell he had just finished with the lady in the basement and now wanted to have me as well, but I was not going to entertain that kind of nonsense. We wrestled for about 20 minutes before he gave up and slumped into a drunkard stupor. Within two minutes, he started snoring.

The following morning, at around 9:00 a.m., when Budda had left, I summoned Ruth, the house help. I asked her to babysit the baby for me while I was getting ready to rush to the mall to make a call. I was quite excited at the idea of fixing Budda, but I was also apprehensive of the outcome. At the gate, I was taken aback to find a stranger manning the gate. As I approached him, I noticed his mean-looking face and piercing eyes were very hostile.

"I'm the new manager here. What do you want?" he asked me coldly. A gateman calling himself a 'manager' was a new one for me.

"This is my house, who are you?" I asked him firmly.

He stifled a chuckle.

"I don't know about that," he said, "All I know is that anyone in this house is a temporary prisoner."

I felt a prickle cut through my belly.

"What do you mean?" I asked incredulously.

"My boss says nobody should leave this house without his express orders to me."

"And who is your boss?"

"The bonafide owner of this house."

"What are his instructions?"

"That nobody leaves here until he says so. He said it is a temporary measure as he sorts out some things."

"I'm his wife, so you can't stop me from leaving and coming whenever I want."

"He didn't talk about a wife; he said 'no one' should go in or out of this gate."

"You will be sorry for this," I said stoically and, turning round, marched back to the house. I was overwhelmed by anger and frustration. I was now sure that I was dealing with a psychopath. All of Budda's actions had no logic. Why was he holding us prisoners? I kept asking myself. Was he planning to kill us all, like he killed Patricia Mode? I knew he was capable of doing any evil.

I went down to the basement to see the lady, Betrice. She was still in bed. I went and sat on the bed.

"Good morning, Betrice," I greeted her, "Did you sleep well?"

She yawned.

"He raped me again…" she said weakly. "I resisted … but he overpowered me."

Chapter 4

Looking at this frightened woman, I felt unfathomable loathing for Budda. I could have killed him, given a chance.

"Please show me the way out; I want to go home," she said miserably.

"I'm sorry … you can't leave … my husband is holding us hostage here."

"What do you mean?" she asked; her voice was so weak that I feared she could suffer a heart attack any minute.

"My husband, the man who kidnapped you, has put us in his custody; he is being helped by a mean stranger manning our gate; I think our usual gatekeeper has been either sacked or killed. I don't know what to make of this madness."

"And the girl who was here last night?"

"She is my house help. She, too, is under custody. He can't let her go; she knows too much. He may end up killing her to silence her once and for all."

"What about us? What will he do with us? Will he kill us, too?"

"I don't think he plans to kill us," I said, trying to soothe her nerves.

"We are now his sex slaves."

She gasped.

"After he gets tired of us, he will kill us to cover his crimes," she said philosophically.

"Yes, you could be right. He is capable of doing exactly that."

"What will we do now?" The despair in her voice was pitiful.

"Together, we must plan our escape."

"Do you think it is possible?"

"Nothing is impossible in this world," I said, but I was not sure I believed what I was saying. The house was surrounded by a 12-foot concrete wall ringed with electric wire. There was no way three desperate women could scale that wall.

We must get out of here, somehow – I believed that part.

"Yes," Betrice said, her voice slightly above a whisper.

"Dress up and come up to the main house we strategize. We have to put the other lady in the loop."

I left her struggling to get out of bed and went back to the main house. I met Ruth waiting for me in the sitting room.

"Madam, what is happening?" she asked anxiously.

"Why, what is up?"

"Boss asked me to make a list of foodstuffs we need for the next one month."

"It is because he has imprisoned us here."

She fidgeted and asked, "Why should he do that?"

"I have no idea."

"Okay then, I'm leaving right away!" she said shrilly.

"You don't understand," I said calmly, "We are already locked up!"

"The doors are not locked!" she continued, "I was outside just now!"

"You can't get out of the gate."

"No, Kimetto can't stop me!" she said excitedly.

"Then go and see for yourself."

She turned and walked hurriedly out of the house. After five minutes or so, she returned, walking and acting like a zombie.

"Kimetto is gone; there is another bad man blocking the gate," she murmured, "He is very rude."

"How do you know that?"

"When I insisted on getting out, he told me if I didn't get out of his sight immediately, he would cut off my breasts to feed his dogs!" she looked pathetic in her misery. "Do you think he can cut off my breasts?"

I had to stifle a chuckle.

"Of course he can't. He was just teasing you so you could leave him alone," I encouraged her.

"He looked dead serious! I can't go out there again."

"I told you so; we are imprisoned here."

"What will we do now?"

"First, prepare that list of foodstuffs. We will need time to plan our escape."

There was a soft knock on the door, and Ruth jumped to her feet and moved swiftly from her seat to hide behind the fridge.

"Come in," I said. There was a momentary pause before the door was slowly pushed open. It was Betrice.

"Come in, please," I told her, "And have a seat."

Ruth emerged from behind the fridge, looking quite flustered.

"Sit down, Ruth," I told her, "And you must now learn to control your nerves. You are behaving like a five-year-old."

"I'm scared of that man outside."

"Forget him, keep away from him, and he won't have any reason to harm you."

She slumped back to her seat. She was visibly frightened. Betrice, on the other hand, looked quite composed.

"Ladies, we are in trouble," I began to address them. But we should keep our cool. There is no need to panic. If we remain calm and united, we shall overcome our troubles."

There was a long silence.

"We must play complacent; we act as if we have resigned ourselves to our fate and pretend we are okay and ready to stay with our tormentor.

Believe it or not, sooner or later, he will lower his guards, and then we will pin him down. I have enough ammunition to finish him if only I can get out of here for just a few minutes."

The two ladies seemed lost in their thoughts; fear and uncertainty overwhelmed them. In their current state of mind, I knew I could not get much help from them. If I was to fix Budda, I had to rely on my own willpower.

"Let us pray to God to get us out of here," Ruth, the house help, offered.

"Yes, we need to pray, but first, we must know why God brought us here in the first place; maybe He wants us to die here," I said.

I was not very religious and found it hard to believe in the power of prayers.

"God forbid!" Ruth interjected, "God wants the best for all of us. He will get us out of here."

"I don't doubt your faith, but I knew of an internationally known preacher who died in an aeroplane crash even after he had vehemently prayed for a safe journey; the plane crashed and killed everybody aboard, including our prayerful preacher. If God has destined us to die here, no amount of prayers will change that."

"Madam, I think Satan is using you to deny us God's mercies."

"No, no, Ruth, I'm not saying praying is bad; I meant prayers should be accompanied by practical solutions."

"No, God does everything for you if you believe in him!" she said with the conviction of a fanatic.

"Okay, Ruth, lead us in prayers, please."

"Thanks, Madam; now, let us close our eyes," she said and then began the longest invocation I had ever endured. After she had exhausted every sacred word in her vocabulary, she concluded with an impassioned entreaty to the apostles.

"I will prepare breakfast," Betrice said, getting to her feet. She had not spoken a word during our short religious discourse.

"I will go and make that foodstuffs list," Ruth also excused herself.

That evening, Budda came home earlier than usual, moderately inebriated. After he had settled down in his favourite seat, he summoned all of us.

"I have called this meeting," he began after we were seated, "to clarify some issues. You are now all under my command and care; from now on, whatever I say is the law. I expect total loyalty from you three. Only when I'm sure of your loyalty will I relax restrictions on your movement.

"Another important thing: don't try any tricks on me. If I catch you playing monkey business with me, I will kill you for sure, and nothing you can do about it. Am I understood?"

Nobody said anything.

"Am I understood?" he yelled. I nodded while the rest responded with a barely audible yes.

"Any questions?" he asked, and again, nobody spoke.

"Okay, if you have no questions, then you can leave."

When the two ladies had left the room, I asked him, "Why are you doing this to me?"

He scowled at me.

"Time for questions is over. I wish to be left alone; I have things to think about."

I left him alone and went back to the bedroom. It was then I made up my mind to bring this madness to an end. Anger and frustrations emboldened me. I was ready to take him head on, but first, I had to have a foolproof plan. I racked my brain until late at night, determined, more than ever before, to emancipate myself from his mistreatment.

The time was shortly before midnight when the silence and peace of the night were suddenly broken by a high-pitched scream coming from somewhere downstairs. I was in my nightwear. I quickly got out of bed and rushed downstairs. The commotion was in Ruth's room. I tiptoed to the door and, straining against the keyhole, heard Ruth say, "Please stop! Don't do this to me, I'm a virgin!"

"I like virgins; today is my lucky day!" Budda growled.

Ruth continued crying as they struggled, then her crying turned into whimpering, and finally, she fell silent. I tried the door handle, but it was locked from inside. A vicious rage cut through my body. It was unbelievable that a man could be this crazy and reckless. This man's actions were not rational at all.

I retreated to the sitting room. I did not turn on the lights. I sat at a vantage position from where I could see Ruth's bedroom. I wanted to see what would happen next. Twenty minutes later, I saw Budda come out, zipping up his pants. He did not look in my direction; he headed straight towards the basement. It was obvious he was going down there to have sex with Betrice; it was her turn. His sick mind had an insatiable desire for sex. It did not make any sense to me, but I knew his days were numbered. I now knew what was to be done and was ready to do it. I went to the kitchen and selected the biggest and sharpest kitchen knife I needed for security. There was no way I would allow that bastard to touch me that night; woe to him if he tried. Back in my bedroom, I locked the door from inside and hid the deadly weapon under my pillow, where I could reach it instantly if the need arose.

I fell asleep only because I knew it was impossible to break the door open without me hearing. I only woke up once at night to breastfeed my baby; I slept deeply. I was awoken by rays of sunlight penetrating through the window curtains and was in time to hear Budda's big car drive out of the compound. I got out of bed and went downstairs. I found Betrice already there, sipping coffee.

"Good morning, Betrice; you are quite early today?"

"He woke me early," she returned.

"Why, what happened?"

"I did as you told us; I pretended all was well," she said airily, "He seemed happy, but that made him quite greedy for me."

"Greedy for your body, not you," I interjected, "He is not capable of liking anyone. Don't be taken in by his false charm."

"I'm not taken," she said, "I pretended; in fact, I hate him!"

Just then, Ruth strolled in, her face puffy and eyes red from crying.

"Good morning, Ruth," I held her shoulders. "What happened? You look really bad," I asked her soothingly. I knew what had happened, but there was no point in letting her know I knew; she would probably blame me for not helping her, not knowing how helpless I was against Budda. I guided her to the seat.

"Tell us what happened."

She broke into heartrending sobbing. She bent her body and buried her face in her hands between her knees.

It was so distressing to see her petite figure being tormented by such emotional pain. I hated Budda for causing her to suffer this much. It was quite heartless for him to do this to her.

Betrice and I just stood there transfixed. She continued sobbing violently. When she was done, she got to her feet and, without uttering a word, walked out. We watched in disbelief as she entered her room.

"Let us go to her," I said.

"Yes," Betrice said breathlessly.

"Follow me," I said, getting to my feet. Unfortunately, we were too late. Ruth had already locked herself in. We tried to persuade her to open the door to no avail; she ignored our pleas. We consoled her from outside the door, but there was no evidence she was listening to us. After we had exhausted ourselves, we dejectedly returned to the sitting room.

"What do you think is the matter with her?" Betrice asked.

"Budda raped her last night," I said softly.

"What! How do you know?"

Chapter 5

"Last night, I heard screams and came downstairs. It was Ruth screaming. I went to her door, but it was locked from the inside. I was able to hear Ruth say – *Please stop! Don't do this to me, I'm a virgin!*" I explained to her, "After he had raped her, I saw him going to the basement, obviously to your bed."

I heard her catch her breath.

"This is unbelievable! Very disgusting!" she said shrilly, "I wish I had never accepted him! That man is surely mad!"

"Yes, he is mad, and that's why we should find a way of stopping him!"

"How do we do that?"

"I have a plan," I said.

She stared at me expectantly and said, "Tell me."

"We know his weakness is alcohol and sex. We will use this to trap him."

"How?"

"Whenever he is drunk, sex seems to put him in a coma. Have you noticed that?"

"Yes."

"So, in his comatose state, we will tie him up with a rope and then lock him up alone in the basement."

"I think that is possible, but what's next?"

"We will let him stay there the whole day, waiting for the man at the gate to come to check on him. When he does, we will tell him that his boss is working there in the basement, and he can go down to see him. If he falls for that and gets down there, I will be ready to lock him up, too. With two of them out of the way, we can get out."

"What if that man at the gate doesn't come to check on him?"

"I shall go to him myself and tell him that the boss wants to see him. I don't think he will refuse to go to see him. We will still achieve the same result."

"What if he locks the gate with a key before leaving the gate unmanned? How will we get out?"

"With the two of them out of the way, we will devise a way out. I want you to continue pretending all is well until we accomplish our mission. Remember, everything must happen in the basement. After he falls asleep, you will wait for me, and together, we will tie him up tightly. This plan is foolproof and involves no risk for us."

Betrice grunted.

"Everything depends on the brute at the gate. If we fail to lure him to the basement, then our plan goes up in smoke."

"I'm almost certain he will come up; don't worry about that."

"So, we have to wait until the day he comes home drunk?"

"Precisely; I'm really looking forward to that day! It will be the beginning of his big fall."

"I still hope that one day, I will wake up and discover this has been just a nightmare."

That day, we had our lunch at 1 p.m., but Ruth did not come out of her room to join us. We tried to knock on her door, but she did not open it. We became extremely anxious when she failed to join us again in the evening for dinner.

Together, we tried to bang on her door and shout her name, but all we got was silence. In a panic, we ran out of the house towards the gate; we needed help to break into the room. But there was nobody at the gate, which was secured with a heavy padlock from inside. For a long moment, we stood there, staring at the imposing gates and the giant padlock, trying to figure out what it all meant. Since it was possible to put the padlock in place from outside the gate, we assumed that the gateman could either be inside the compound or outside.

Then, suddenly, there was lightning in the sky, followed by a thunderstorm, and heavy raindrops had already begun falling. As we stood there, I was mesmerized by the sudden change of weather and circumstances; it was then I remembered there was a window in Ruth's room that could be accessed from behind the house. I beckoned Betrice to follow me as I ran round the house. We reached the window almost at the same time.

The curtains were partly drawn, and the room was in partial darkness. The first thing that hit me was the empty bed.

"She is not here!" Betrice exclaimed.

I did not say anything. As my eyes became accustomed to the darkness, I was able to see a human figure in the open wardrobe.

"There is someone in the wardrobe," I said, straining my eyes to see more.

"Oooh, no! My God!" Betrice wailed, "She's in the wardrobe; she hanged herself!"

I could also make out the complete picture; she had hung herself using a bed sheet. She was still in the clothes she wore that morning; her mouth hung open, but her eyes were closed. I was suddenly gripped by an intense fear of the unknown. Another thunderstorm roared, and rain began to fall more intensely. Then suddenly, the thought of my baby, who was alone in the house, came to me, and I ran madly towards the house with Betrice on my heels. I found him crying softly. I gathered him into my hands, and after suckling him for a minute or so, he was back to his peaceful sleep.

The sound of rain beating against the roof and window panes was deafening.

"I'm scared," Betrice said. I strained to hear what she was saying, "We are all alone in this big house, with a dead body downstairs. I wonder where her angry spirit is now; it could be here with us in this room!"

Another violent thunderstorm made us reach out to each other for comfort. It was very scary. We held each other tightly as yet another lightning lighted up the room.

"I'm sure it is her angry spirit raging against this house," she said.

"I'm now also scared. I wonder where that gateman is and what game they are playing with us. This house has now claimed the lives of two women."

I felt Betrice's body jerk.

"What do you mean by lives of two women?" she asked shakily, "Who is the other woman?"

"It was a girl Budda brought here some time ago. I don't know what happened, but a couple of days ago, I saw him loading her body in his car boot. He killed her down there in the basement, in the same room you are staying in now."

I felt her heart kick violently against my chest.

"Why didn't you tell me about this?"

"How could it have helped you? I didn't find it important to tell you; it could have only made your life more miserable."

"I think this man is the devil himself. I'm starting to think we will not leave this house alive." Her voice was shaky with fear.

"Let us be positive; negativity will only stress us. Remember, we have a plan to defeat him. Keep that hope burning," I said.

The wind and rain outside intensified, threatening to uproot trees and everything. Their roar was ferocious and quite frightening. It was the scariest night of my life. It was around eleven o'clock when suddenly, the lights went off, resulting in a total blackout. An impenetrable darkness engulfed the house, which made Beatrice scream.

"God, have mercy on us," she said, gripping me more tightly. I could hear her laboured breathing but could not see her.

The sound of heavy footsteps coming upstairs paralyzed us with terror. Then, just outside the bedroom door, the sound of the footsteps died, and we expected a knock at the door, or the door to open, but nothing such happened. It seemed whoever was out there was not in a hurry to come in. After ten unnerving minutes, the door creaked, paused and then creaked again. By that time, I was nearly having a heart attack; my heart was beating so violently that I could feel my chest pounding. It was obvious that whoever was opening the door had evil intentions. We waited, but there was nothing but silence. Darkness pressed hard on us. Heavy breathing just next to us made me realize someone was already in the room. Suddenly, Betrice jumped to her feet, screaming in panic, and I also began screaming. As I sprang to my feet, I bumped into someone standing next to me; I instinctively fought him wildly, scratching out with my nails. Betrice continued screaming, and then, mercifully, the lights came back, lighting up the room. It was the cruel gateman tormenting us.

"What are you doing here?" I screamed at him.

He grunted.

"Ladies, calm down; I'm here to check on you," he said in a shaky voice, "It is my duty to make sure you are safe!"

"You are lying!" I shouted at him, "You are here to harm us! What is your mission? To kill or to rape us?"

The mirth in his face made him look even more sinister.

"No, no; I'm neither a killer nor a bad man; I am just doing my job."

"Do you know there is a dead woman downstairs?" I asked him.

That startled him.

"What? ... A dead woman?" he stammered.

"Ruth, the house-help is dead."

"What happened to her?"

"We don't know; she apparently committed suicide."

"Why the hell did she kill herself?"

"What are you going to do about it?"

"About what?"

"You have a dead woman in your hands; you have just said it is your duty to keep us safe."

"If she wanted to die, then that was her business, not mine."

"What about her body? It has to be moved."

"I'm not a morgue attendant!" he said frantically, "I'm going back to the gate; you deal with her body." Saying that, he hurriedly walked out of the room. One could tell he was also scared to be in this haunted house.

Mysteriously, Budda did not turn up that night, and the rain continued all night long.

In the morning, I went to the gateman to enquire if he knew where Budda was and what he was going to do about the body in the house. The gateman peered at me as I approached him.

"Good morning; I have come to enquire if you know where your boss is."

"Why should I know that? I'm not his keeper."

"Okay, what do you plan to do about the body in the house?"

"If the ayah wanted to die, then let her stay dead; just don't involve me."

"Then call the police."

He looked up sharply, giving me what I would have described as an incredulous stare.

"Don't you know your husband has a phobia for cops? He says that policemen and women are the source of all suffering in this country. Now, forget about the police and go back to the house. Your husband will know what to do with the corpse in the house."

I felt so dejected that I had nothing more to say to him.

That evening, Budda turned up at around eight O'clock, tipsy as usual. He summoned Betrice and me for what he called 'serious' talk in the living room.

"What happened to her?" he started with his guttural voice.

"We don't know," I responded, "When she failed to turn up for lunch and supper yesterday, we decided to check on her and found her dead in the wardrobe, although in the morning, she looked quite depressed."

"Okay, now listen and listen really well. She left here four days ago to visit her parents but never returned. That is the story; that is what happened to her as far as you are concerned. If any of you contradicts this story, you two will go to jail for a long time."

"We didn't kill her! Why should we go to jail?" I asked, shocked by his assertion.

He cleared his throat.

"The detectives are quite complicated; if a body is found in a house, the owner of the house and whoever was in the house when the death occurred are the main suspects."

"But she committed suicide; why don't we just tell them the truth? We are all innocent," I interjected.

"We are innocent but suspects!" he said impatiently, "The police would like to know the circumstance under which she died. They may as well suspect you murdered her; you had a motive."

I felt my heart lurch.

"What motive? We didn't have any motive to murder her."

"I know you didn't, but, as I said, detectives are very complicated; they come up with all crazy ideas. They may suspect you killed her because you thought I was about to make her my third wife. Any clever prosecutor will buy that story. That is why I want to protect you."

I felt sick.

"But that is ridiculous!"

"To you, it is, but to the police, it makes a lot of sense."

"I think you are making a big deal out of a straight forward thing." It was Betrice, saying something for the first time.

"It may seem that way to you now, but it will be different when the police come for you."

"What do you plan to do about the body?"

"I will get rid of it; they will never find it."

"Well, that is your burden, but can you tell us why you are detaining us here against our will?"

"I'm holding you here for your own good and safety. Both of you are my wives, but I don't trust you will behave well if I let you go wherever you want. One day, when you win my confidence, I will let you go. But until then, you stay here and serve me, your husband."

"My people must be searching for me; I need to get in touch with them," Betrice said, "You must let me go!"

"Write them a note telling them that you got married and are fine and enjoying your life with your new husband. I will have it delivered. I think you should do the same, Shiro. Let your people know you are fine and happy and will visit them soon when you get an opportunity."

"I will not write anything to anyone," I said defiantly.

"Me, too!" Betrice also declared and added, "You must let us go!"

"You can please yourselves," Budda said dismissively, "Tonight, you must help me get the body out through the backdoor."

"Over my dead body!" I exclaimed.

"Count me out, too!" Betrice said vehemently.

Budda sighed.

"That is why I can't let you out of here, because I know you are two spineless bitches waiting to betray me!" he said angrily, "Whatever I saw in any of you beats me. Sometimes, I think I need my head to be examined by a good headshrinker." He got to his feet and walked out of the room.

"Now you see why we should execute our plan as soon as possible," I said to Betrice, "He is determined to detain us here forever and use us as his sex slaves. We must overpower him before he does something sinister to us."

"I can't stop thinking of what happened to Ruth," Betrice said, "To be raped and have nowhere to report the crime is the worst kind of violation! That torture drove her to end her life."

"You are right, but let us now think about our own survival. If we don't do something about it, we may end up like her!"

"Do you think we will succeed?" she asked uneasily.

"I have no doubt," I assured her, "The way I have planned it, it is foolproof."

"So, when do you want us to do it?"

"As I told you, there are conditions to this plan to make it work. First, he must be drunk; second, he must be in the basement. It is your part to inform me when he is in one of those alcohol-induced sleeps."

She nodded.

"Okay, I will do that at the right time."

"Good, now it is just a matter of time."

I was now very optimistic that my plan to bring down Budda would work. I wanted justice for Patricia, the girl he murdered in the basement, and Ruth, our house help, who committed suicide after a horrendous rape ordeal in his hands. I also needed justice for myself for all the mental pain he had caused me.

Chapter 6

When everyone had gone to bed, I remained in the sitting room, waiting to see how Budda would deal with Ruth's body. I knew he would act that night. I sat at my favourite seat, facing Ruth's Room. From my position, I could see who went in or out of the room. I pretended to be watching the TV, but my mind was not on it at all. I tuned to CNN International so that if Budda came in and asked me what I was doing there that late in the night, I could tell him that I was following the unfolding events in the US after the shooting of President Ronald Reagan.

The sitting room was in darkness, safe from the light coming from the television. At around 2:00 a.m., I saw Budda emerge from the basement. I watched as he opened Ruth's door using his spare key. He turned on the light, and I heard him curse loudly. After a few minutes, I heard a loud thud, which I assumed was the body that had fallen from the wardrobe to the floor.

It was a moment of intense suspension as I waited to see him emerge with the body. After about ten minutes or so, he came out without the body; he looked dejected, and with his head bent forward, he disappeared into the basement. Five minutes later, as I was about to give up, he reappeared, this time carrying what looked like a tool. He went back to Ruth's room, and this time, he locked the door from inside. After what seemed an eternity, I heard the sound of the door lock turning, and a moment later, Budda emerged, carrying a big plastic carrier bag on his back.

I was surprised because there was no way an adult human body could fit in that plastic bag. It looked quite heavy, but the body could not fit in there. So, what was he carrying in that bag?

Then, as nature would have it, the heavy bag burst open, spilling its contents onto the floor. What followed was like what you see in horror movies. It was so horrifying that I had to cover my mouth with my hands to stop myself from screaming. I knew if Budda knew I knew his secret, he would definitely kill me.

The first to pop out of the burst bag was Ruth's head; it hit the floor first and then began rolling towards the sitting room. I knew it was her head because it had the same hairstyle she had when I last saw her. The scene was macabre, with blood and body parts strewn everywhere. Overwhelmed, I went to the sofa settee and lay down; I had seen enough for one day. I must have passed out because the next time I woke up, it was daytime. My baby was yelling upstairs. I quickly got to my feet and ran upstairs to my bedroom. He was okay but very hungry. As I suckled him, the images of last night flooded my mind, and I felt sick.

Finally, when I went downstairs, I found Betrice in the kitchen, preparing breakfast. The corridor outside

Ruth's office looked neat; I was baffled by how Budda managed to clean up the mess.

"Have you seen Budda?" I asked her.

"No, I thought he was with you," she returned.

"No, he must have slept in the spare bedroom at the corner in the basement."

"Maybe, I don't know. Do you think he got rid of Ruth's body?"

Again, I felt sick.

"I think he did, but not in the manner you would have expected."

"What do you mean?"

"I mean, he had the guts to cut her body into pieces and then stuff the pieces into a plastic bag. Can you imagine that?"

"What! That is really evil! That man is a devil! Who does that to another human's body? I think he has a psychiatric disorder."

"I learned that a long time ago."

"And what are you still doing with him?"

"By the time I realized it," I said sorrowfully, "It was too late to leave, but that was then; now I'm very much ready to leave!"

"By the way, how did you know he cut her body into pieces?"

"The bag burst open as he carried it out of Ruth's room, spilling everything onto the floor. It still baffles me how he cleaned that mess. There were blood stains and body parts everywhere."

"What did you do after seeing that horrific scene?

"I passed out on the sofa settee; I just awoke this morning."

"What do we do now? Living in the same house with a man capable of such a grisly act is like relaxing in a pool with a killer crocodile swimming around in the pool!"

"The sooner we execute our plan, the better for us."

"I hope it happens tonight!"

"Me, too."

But it did not happen. Budda went missing for three consecutive nights, but his henchman at the gate was still there.

When Budda finally came home, he behaved like a demented bully. We were relaxing in the sitting room when he trudged in.

"Can I have a glass of whisky," he demanded.

I went to the cabinet and poured him the whisky.

"I hope you haven't poisoned it; I know you two have been plotting to kill me, but you can't succeed. I'm too smart for you two."

"Not everybody is a killer; nobody wants to kill you," I said sarcastically.

"I just want you to know I know your plan, but I will finish you long before you even attempt." He banged the table with his fist.

"I said nobody wants to kill you," I said calmly.

"How dare you talk while I'm still talking!" he shouted, "You two now know too much to be let free ever again!"

"We know nothing," Betrice tried to calm him.

"Shut up, you woman!" he yelled at her.

"Can't you learn to keep your mouth shut when I'm talking? Don't you realize that your miserable lives are now in my hands? You two must keep me occupied and happy; otherwise, if I get bored, I will get rid of you! By the way, I want you two to know that I collected each of you from the roadside, so to me, you are trash!"

He pushed the glass across the table towards me.

"Get me another drink!" he snapped at me.

I went to the cabinet and poured him another drink. He gulped half of it at once.

"Now, you two go to your rooms and wait for me!" he bellowed, "Tonight, I need real action!"

We remained seated.

"I said get out of here now! Go to your rooms!" he ranted, "Don't you have ears?"

Cowed, we got to our feet and left the room. I was so scared that my whole body started trembling. I could see Betrice was also in the same sorry state. I went upstairs, and she went to the basement to wait for what fate had in store for us. There is nothing worse in this world than waiting for someone who is hell-bent to destroy you. The fear, hate and loathing were suffocating me. The thought of sleeping with him made me really sick.

By the time he came up to the bedroom, I was completely numb; I had zero feelings for anything. If I had the strength, I could have killed him on that day, in fact, that moment.

As he fumbled with his clothes, I managed to blot out everything. He joined me in the bed, but by then, I was as cold as death itself. I just lay there, waiting for him to finish whatever he was doing. When he was done, he rolled away from me, cursing. He got out of bed and began to put on his clothes again. As he dressed, he threw at me some lewd insults. I just ignored him.

About two hours later, I felt someone trying to wake me up by tapping me softly on my shoulder.

"Wake up! Quickly! He is dead asleep!" someone whispered excitedly. I was momentarily disoriented, and then I realized that it was Betrice calling me.

I hurriedly got out of bed and put on my slacks.

"Let's go," I said. The excitement of the moment had also got up with me. The moment of truth was here; it was the hour of reckoning. We ran downstairs. We were lucky to find two strong ropes at the store, but still, we needed a strong cello tape to seal his big mouth. I remembered seeing a cello tape on the bookshelf in the sitting room. We went there and found it. Excitedly, we ran down into the basement and found Budda still dead asleep, snoring deeply. I pushed the blanket aside, uncovering him; he was completely naked.

"Tie up his legs while I do the arms and midriff," I ordered Betrice.

"Okay, no problem," she returned, picking one of the ropes.

"Make sure you tighten the rope well; we can't afford any mistakes at this stage."

"Don't worry about that; I have him," she said in a matter-of-factly style. I knew she was up to the task, and I had nothing to worry about. I picked up my rope and began to tie him up, but it was not as easy as I had thought. When we were done tying him up, we stood back to see what we had accomplished. He looked well-secured. Betrice had done a better job than me. His legs were so tightly tied that I feared he would develop thrombosis.

"Seal his mouth, but leave his nose open," I told her.

She snapped up the tape and expertly placed it across his mouth. When she was done, she gave him a soft pat on the back of his neck.

"Let us get out of here," I said, leading the way out. I locked the basement door and put the key in my pocket.

"Let us go back to my bedroom," I told her, "We have nothing more to do tonight."

"Now, everything depends on what the gateman will do," Betrice said as we climbed the stairs.

"Yes, but don't worry about it, I have him," I said, copying her phrase.

In the morning, around 9.00 a.m., we went down to the basement to see how Budda was fairing. We found him still lying on the bed just as we had left him, only this time he was awake. His face was distorted by fear, hate and anger. Sweat beads covered his forehead.

The anger and hate in his eyes when he saw us were visibly evident. I removed the cello tape from his mouth; I wanted to hear what he had to say in his hour of defeat.

"Who did this to me!" he yelled at us.

"We did," I said confidently.

"Are you crazy? Untie me now, or I will kill you!" he went on yelling.

"You are now under our command," I said, standing next to the bed, "Your evil deeds have caught up with you."

"You don't know what you're doing; you will never get out of here alive; Kingangi, my gateman, will never let you get out of here. He has my instructions to kill you should anything happen to me!"

"He is working with us now," I mocked him.

He chuckled.

"Never; Kingangi can never work with losers like you two! You are lying. If he doesn't see me in the next couple of hours, he will come to finish you, but you can save yourself by releasing me immediately. I will accept your apology."

"The blood of the young lady you murdered right here is crying for justice."

"You devil, what are you saying?" he shouted, straining against the ropes.

"You will regret this madness you are committing!"

It was then I remembered there was a secret door in the basement leading to the grounds behind the house. How could I have forgotten it! I wondered.

"Where is the secret door you used to get the girl's body outside the house?"

"I don't know what you are talking about!" There was no confidence in his voice; he looked defeated.

"Stop denying it!" I shook him with my hand; I saw you carrying her body to the boot of your car! Show us that door!"

He sneered at me.

"Go to hell, you bitch! I will not show you… I said you will not get out of here alive. Now get out of my sight!"

"Let us look for it, Betrice." Finding the hidden backdoor proved harder than I envisaged. It took us two hours to locate the door. It was cleverly disguised by the finishing and decorations of the wall across its surface. It had no handle but a small keyhole. When I returned to the basement bedroom, Budda was still in the same position, looking scared and desperate. His eyes radiated murderous rage.

"I tell you, you won't get away with this silly plot of yours!' he said in a subdued voice.

"We will see," I said, going through his suit pockets for his keys. I found a bunch of keys and went back to the door, where Betrice was waiting anxiously. The fifth key in the bunch slipped into the lock readily. I turned it, pushed the door a little, and it started to open outwardly. Betrice heaved a sigh of relief. I closed the door and relocked it.

"Let us search all these rooms for a spare key," I told her, "I don't want to make another mistake; I nearly forgot about that damned door."

After searching everywhere, we were able to ascertain that there was no spare key of any kind hidden anywhere in all the rooms in the basement. I cello taped his mouth again.

Chapter 6

"Let us get out of here," I told Betrice.

I locked the main basement door, and then we retreated to the sitting room to wait for the gateman to react if, indeed, he was going to react.

At around 2 p.m., the doorbell rang.

"It is him!" Betrice whispered excitedly, gesturing.

"Let me handle him," I said, getting to my feet.

I opened the main door.

"Yes, what can I do for you?" I asked him steadily.

"Where is the boss? I haven't seen him since morning."

"He is working in his basement room. Do you want to go and see him?"

"If he is working, then there is no need to disturb him," he said resignedly. "I only found it odd for the boss to remain in the house all day, but if he is working, I have nothing more to say." He turned and walked away, leaving me staring after him. I closed and locked the door.

"He is not suspicious of anything," I said, sitting down in my seat.

"Do you think he will accept to go down there alone?"

"I'm sure he will," I said confidently, "He will soon go down there."

"You sound so sure of yourself."

"Yes, because I'm sure."

After two hours, I unlocked the basement door and headed to the gate; the gateman eyed me uneasily as I approached.

"The boss is asking for you?" I said to him.

"What does he want?"

"He didn't tell me."

He hesitated for a long moment.

"I'll go and see him," he said, getting down his high stool. He ascertained the gate was securely locked and then headed towards the main house. I followed him. He walked briskly. He went straight into the basement. As soon as he got to the bottom of the short staircase, I closed and locked the door.

"What are you doing?" I heard him shout. A few minutes later, I heard him pounding on the door, cursing. Betrice joined me.

"It is done!" I said excitedly.

"What do we do now?" she asked breathlessly.

"Let's go to the police!" I said.

Outside the gate, there was a road, relatively busy with vehicles, but human traffic was quite sparse. When we got to the gate, Betrice asked, "What now?"

"We will keep screaming until someone notices."

We started screaming at the top of our voices like we were under attack. After three minutes, there was a loud pounding on the gate, and we realized that someone was outside the gate.

"Get to the police! Quickly!" I yelled.

"What is going on?" a male voice asked from the other side of the gate.

"We are under attack! Please get to the police!"

"Okay … Okay. Take care!" he said.

We went on screaming, and it seemed like a lot of people had gathered outside the gate. A woman outside the gate joined us in screaming.

A moment later, the siren of a police car filled the air, and a few minutes later, the sound of tortured wheels announced the police's arrival.

"Police! Please open this gate!" a policeman said loudly, using a megaphone.

"The attackers have locked the gate! They are in the main house!" I shouted back. The crowd outside began murmuring.

Within a few minutes, a uniformed police officer appeared on top of the gate, climbed down like an expert, and landed safely and silently.

"Quiet, ladies! The police are here!" he calmed us; he was armed with an AK-47 machine gun. We stopped screaming.

From his pocket, he produced a tong-like tool which he used to cut the gate's heavy padlock. The police, some in uniform and others in civilian clothes, poured into the compound. From there on, it was a hive of activity. Betrice and I remained at the gate, waiting.

About twenty minutes later, the gateman appeared, handcuffed, followed by Budda without handcuffs. In their wake was a policewoman carrying my baby.

"Ladies, tell us what happened," a police officer donning an inspector's uniform told us.

I told him my story in summary, and he listened to me attentively. When I was done and Betrice had collaborated on my story, he ordered a junior policeman to handcuff Budda as well.

Two days later, Budda was arraigned in court, charged with the murder of Patricia Mode, and the kidnapping of Betrice Memet. He was also charged with holding three women hostage, and finally, he was accused of unlawfully disposing of a human body.

When the charges were read to him, he denied all of them. He pleaded to be released on bond, but the prosecution vehemently opposed this, saying he would likely interfere with witnesses if he was let free. The trial judge agreed with the prosecution and ordered that the accused must remain in custody until the determination of his case.

After four years of hearing the case, the Judge found Budda guilty of all the charges and convicted him accordingly. He was handed two life sentences.